THE BRITISH LIBRARY

TREASURES
IN FOCUS

Decorated Papers
The Olga Hirsch Collection

LEFT The fold visible at the centre of this gold-embossed sheet shows that it was once used as the end leaves of a book.

THE OLGA HIRSCH COLLECTION of decorated papers at the British Library has been described as one of the largest and most remarkable collections of such items in the world.

Decorated papers appear unnoticed all around us; they feature in various items of stationery, they line cabinets, wrap gifts, back playing cards, and adorn interiors in the form of wallpaper. No one can pinpoint exactly when people began to decorate paper, but it seems likely that techniques developed soon after the Chinese invention of paper around the second century BC. Knowledge of various methods for decorating paper then spread westwards: marbling, for example, recorded in China in the tenth century, found its way to Japan by the twelfth century and from there spread to Turkey and Persia by the thirteenth and fourteenth centuries respectively. Europe saw its first imported marbled papers two centuries later, and by the seventeenth century, Germany and France had begun to make their own, aided by the publication of 'recipe' books which described methods and techniques.

Some countries developed unique ways of decorating papers, such as the metallic papers produced in eighteenth-century Germany. Other techniques – for example, woodblock printing – were more widely employed, though with stylistic variations. Italy was a producer of pictorial block prints in the late fifteenth and early sixteenth centuries, an industry which flourished again in the eighteenth and nineteenth centuries. The Netherlands was also a manufacturer, though it was more important as a trade centre of import and export. A specific design – a gold-embossed floral pattern on a multicoloured background – even became known as 'Dutch gilt', because of its trade connections with the Netherlands, though it was actually made in Germany. Even within an individual country, centres of production could be numerous, for example Augsburg, Nuremberg and Fürth in Germany and Paris, Rouen and Orleans in France. The demand was huge, and many workers were employed to satisfy it.

As early as the fifteenth century, the poorer sections of society used woodblock printed images to adorn their homes, just as the rich used tapestries and paintings. It is the book trade, however, which has

always provided the major market for decorated papers. Until the nineteenth century, many books were not sold ready-bound but were wrapped in cheap protective covers, frequently made of decorated paper. Once the purchase had been made, the customer then decided if it was worth the expense of having the work bound in a more robust leather binding. In the eighteenth century, decorated paper often featured as part of a permanent binding particularly for inexpensive books given as gifts, including almanacs, diaries and calendars and popular novels. Some books routinely had paper covers, usually works which had an unusual format, for example music scores, play scripts, sermons, letters and dissertations.

OPPOSITE This eighteenth-century paper from the Netherlands exhibits a dotted background. These marks are made by metal pins being driven into the wood block and are frequently found in so-called 'Cotton' papers (see p. 18).

Whether the covering was to be temporary or permanent, it was important for the design to be attractive to draw the attention of customers, and there were many methods of decoration, the use of block printing, coloured paste, metal leaf and marbling being the most common in Europe. Such techniques were sometimes combined, although the more sophisticated the methods employed, the more expensive the paper would be. Sometimes, after the basic outline was block printed, colours would be added by hand.

Perhaps the most common use for decorated paper within the book trade was as end leaves in books. As well as looking attractive, these papers had the practical purpose of concealing the structural features of the binding, for example the supports on which the books were sewn, and acting as a buffer for any dye which might leak out from the leather covers.

With the advent of the Industrial Revolution, methods of production were mechanised causing designs to appear somewhat flat and lifeless. It seems that paper makers were aware of the problem and large factories like Buntpapierfabrik A.G. of Aschaffenburg in Germany employed craftsmen, one of whom was the bookbinder Paul Kersten (1865-1943), who was permitted to experiment in an attempt to add individualism to the patterns.

OPPOSITE Block-printed paper was a cheap and easy way to make ready-bound books, in particular diaries and almanacs, more attractive. The slip case lined with decorated paper makes the diary featured here especially suitable as a gift.

In recent times, artists and craftsmen have recognised the value of decorating papers by hand. The Hirsch collection has examples of the work of artist Tirzah Ravilious (1908-51, wife of Eric Ravilious), paper book covers produced by the Penguin Company, Turkish flower marbled patterns by Necmeddin Okyay (1885-1976) from Istanbul, and Sydney Cockerell (1906-87) of the famous binding workshop Douglas Cockerell & Son.

OPPOSITE Mame of Tours specialised in producing popular paper-bound novels. This book is part of the *Bibliothèque de la jeunesse Chrétienne* series, which were sometimes given as Sunday School prizes.

RIGHT Woodblock on paste paper. Note the veining on the background colours which is characteristic of such paper.

The motifs used on decorated papers, while having no pretensions towards 'high art', are colourful and frequently amusing, investing the most pedestrian objects with an appeal that is accessible to all.

The Hirsch collection contains many other types of decoration including brush coating, sprinkling, spraying and Japanese Katagami work, a traditional method of making paper stencils.

OPPOSITE Katagami, a stencil-cutting art, originated in Japan in the eighth century. Later, in the nineteenth century, intricately cut sheets similar to this were made from mulberry paper and were exported to France and England where they proved a great influence on the art world.

OLGA HIRSCH

Olga Hirsch, née Ladenburg, came from a prominent family in Frankfurt where her father was President of the Chamber of Commerce. In 1911, she married Paul Adolf Hirsch (1881-1951) who ran Hirsch and Company, iron manufacturers. They had two sons and two daughters.

The Hirsch family were keen collectors. Paul's older brother Robert amassed a famous art collection and Paul himself built up a library of rare music scores and musical literature which he made available to researchers. Olga Hirsch trained as a bookbinder in order to conserve this material. She was particularly intrigued by the highly decorated paper wrappers which covered some of the music scores and began to research and collect them for herself.

The dangerous political situation in Germany in 1936 convinced the Hirsch family that they should leave Frankfurt. They settled in Cambridge where

Paul continued to work on his music library (which was sold to the British Museum in 1946), and Olga began to catalogue her growing collection, which formed the basis of the standard work on decorated papers, *Buntpapier* (Decorated Paper) by Albert Haemmerle, published in Munich in 1961.

Examples of most types of decorated paper can be found in the collection, which was arranged both by technique and then chronologically. However, it proved impossible for her to determine precise details due to the lack of physical evidence. The papers were no longer attached to the books in which they were used and manufacturers did not always 'sign' their papers.

As well as 3,500 sheets of decorated papers, the collection includes around 150 books which contained decorated paper, a reference library, and extensive files covering acquisitions processes.

BLOCK-PRINTED PAPERS were produced throughout the world. The technique was relatively simple and paper decorated in this way could be produced in large quantities even though the designs were impressed by hand.

The blocks, usually wood, featured raised designs which were then covered with inks or watercolours and pressed onto the surface to be decorated. For reasons of economy, the blocks were also used to decorate materials other than paper, particularly fabric. Some designs were even called 'Cotton paper' because they were used on both cloth and paper. Mrs Hirsch wrote, 'It is known that in Alsace, Augsburg, Vienna, Venice and Holland block prints on paper were produced at the same factory which stamped fabrics. Even honey bread was baked and stamped at some of the factories, thus getting the greatest possible use out of the blocks. This bread was wrapped in decorated paper, similar to that used for Nuremberg toys, and thus customs duty, which is said to have been very high, was avoided.'

PREVIOUS PAGES German block-printed papers frequently featured pastoral scenes.

Perhaps the most prolific exponents of this technique were the French decorated paper makers of the eighteenth century. Many firms emerged in Paris, Orleans, Rouen and Tournai. Helpfully for researchers, manufacturers' details and pattern number are often printed at the edge of the sheets! In the nineteenth and twentieth centuries, the Japanese made block-printed paper of superb quality and the craft is still practised there today.

ABOVE The light-hearted nature of some patterns makes them particularly suitable for children's books.

OPPOSITE This Italian sixteenth-century sheet features the Church Fathers, which would have been a very suitable design for the contents: tracts by the priest and religious reformer, Savanarola, 1512-17.

RIGHT The French trade in decorated printed paper dated back to the sixteenth century but was given a boost by the invention of wallpaper featuring a continuous design by Jean Papillon (1661-1723). This hand-coloured wallpaper is signed, and was printed and numbered by 'Les Associées', Papillon's neighbour in the Rue St Jacques in Paris.

LEFT AND BELOW These motifs are from a paper that was block-printed in black and hand-painted.

OPPOSITE Publishers attracted custom by employing bold designs and unusual features, as in this eighteenth-century woodblock wrapper, which has a space for the owner's name to be added.

Des Livres
de la Bibliotheque de
M.

ABOVE The block-printed end leaves on this highly decorated nineteenth-century vellum binding have been personalised by the addition of a heart shape.

OPPOSITE This nineteenth-century Japanese block print demonstrates a mastery of design.

OPPOSITE Designs with strong vertical lines were particularly suitable for wallpaper. Binders would also use this type of design, cutting as much paper as was needed for end leaves in books.

RIGHT This repeated floral motif blocked on paper would also be suitable for use on fabric.

ABOVE AND OPPOSITE
Block printing is a
surprisingly versatile
technique. Contrast the
delicacy of the design
above with the bold pattern
opposite. Both papers
are Japanese.

IN EIGHTEENTH-CENTURY Germany, paper makers specialised in sheets decorated with gold and silver. There were several methods, the more traditional featuring a woodblock design printed on coloured paper using a varnish-like metallic ink. Embossed papers were made by impressing metal leaf into the surface using engraved panels. Designs were cut either in relief or intaglio and pressed onto previously coloured paper. Official permission from the local council had to be obtained before metal papers could be manufactured and these privileges were bought and sold. Several paper-decorating families and firms were interconnected, for example, Georg Christoph Stoy married the sister of the paper maker Jacob Enderlin (and she was also the widow of paper marbler Mathais Frölich).

Gold and silver decorated papers were expensive to produce. This type of decoration was often used on labels, tags, invitations and visiting cards. New techniques developed in the nineteenth century meant that colours could more easily be incorporated into embossed designs to appeal to the taste for elaborate decoration.

PREVIOUS PAGES Floral patterns are the most common decorative scheme, with the design varying from maker to maker. This one is signed by Johann Michael Schwibecher of Augsburg.

ABOVE Georg Christoph Stoy of Augsburg (b.1670) produced a wide range of papers, including this delicate metallic varnish paper.

The metallic paper trade became so successful that it supported several German family firms. One of these belonged to Paul Reymund. According to the Nuremberg register of pattern makers, Reymund (d.1815) was a master practitioner.

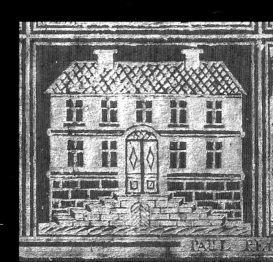

BELOW Sheets printed with the alphabet and with
numbers were often used for teaching. This example
was blocked by Johann Georg Eckart of Nuremberg.

LEFT This floral gold-embossed sheet from Augsburg is by Johann Michael Munck, whose father was a paper marbler and whose son was an embosser.

BELOW This educational
sheet has been decorated
with the letters of the
alphabet and their
associated images.

OPPOSITE A floral pattern
signed by Johann Paul
Schindler of Fürth.

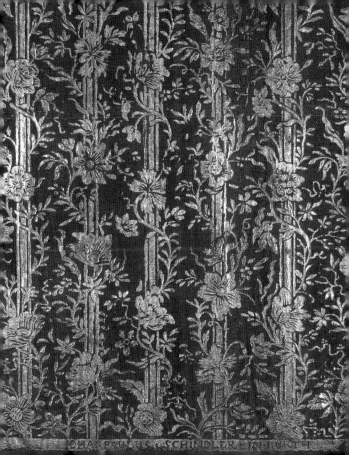

OPPOSITE Embossed
sheets frequently
featured religious scenes,
particularly those
involving saints and
evangelists. This
enlargement shows
Matthew proudly
displaying his Gospel,
which looks as if it were
also bound in gold-
embossed paper!

OPPOSITE Chinese motifs reflected contemporary interest in the East, as shown in this metallic paper from 1730.

ABOVE This mid-nineteenth-century label demonstrates how paper could now be blocked with colour as well as gold.

THIS METHOD INVOLVES pigments being dropped onto size, a glutinous substance which floats on a bath of water. Patterns are drawn in the colours, by means of combs and other implements, or using chemicals such as turpentine. When a sheet of paper is laid on the surface, the pattern transfers to the paper. It appears the technique began in the East and was known in China as early as the tenth century. By the sixteenth century, marbled papers were being imported into Europe and became very popular. In Germany, sheets of marbled paper were bound to use as autograph books.

European craftsmen were keen to produce their own versions rather than spend money on imports. In Amsterdam, Gerard ter Brugghen published instructions for marbling in 1616. During the seventeenth century, Germany became proficient in the technique, followed by France where royal binder Mace Ruette (d.1644) was credited with the invention! The English were late in adopting the practice but once it became established, popularised by the seventeenth-century diarist John Evelyn's lecture to the Royal Society, marbled paper became the favoured choice for end leaves in books.

Demand increased and in the nineteenth century, new printing techniques developed to mechanise the process. Marbling workshops still exist (and many important artists and bookbinders have contributed to the craft) but they tend to cater to the needs of hand bookbinders since they are not able to supply papers in bulk.

PREVIOUS PAGES This pattern, French curl, was particularly admired in France and began to be made in the 1660s.

ABOVE In seventeenth-century Germany, marbled papers were commonly used in the production of the album amicorum, or autograph book, such as this example from 1605.

RIGHT Combs and implements resembling rakes were used to draw the colours into each other.

_Pl. I_

ABOVE There was intense popular interest in how marbled papers were made, and methods of production were described and illustrated in Denis Diderot's, *Encyclopédie* (Paris, 1751-65), vol XXIX. Plates I & II relate to the article 'Marbreur de Papier'.

OPPOSITE Other techniques like stencilling contributed to the decorative process.

OPPOSITE Certain patterns became so well known that they were given names, and methods of making them were described in recipe books. This pattern is called 'Bouquet'.

ABOVE Nineteenth-century English bookbinders made much use of marbled end leaves. This pattern featuring 'waves' of colour is called Spanish marble and originated in seventeenth-century Spain. This example was employed by the London binder, Charles Hering.

LEFT Industrialisation in the nineteenth century caused patterns to look somewhat 'flat', as illustrated by this paper decorated with a design called 'Nonpareil'.

OPPOSITE This enlargement shows the vibrancy of nineteenth-century hand-marbled patterns.

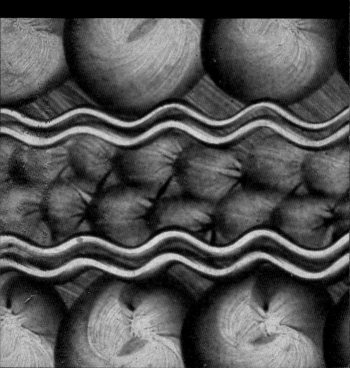

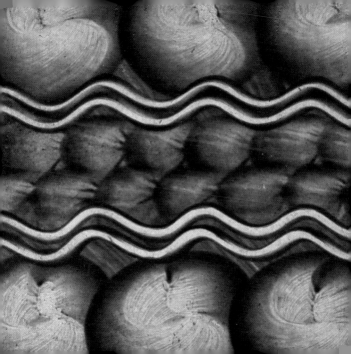

PASTE PAPERS, most commonly produced in eighteenth-century Germany, involved coloured paste (frequently red and blue) being brushed over sheets, and decoration applied with combs, wood blocks, binders' tools and even the thumb. Sometimes these papers are known as 'Herrnhuter Papiere' after the Herrnhut religious brotherhood in Saxony who produced many examples.

Paste papers were the quickest, easiest and cheapest way for a bookbinder to produce decorated papers. Skill and specialist equipment were required for block printing, embossing and marbling but a binder could produce paste papers himself.

PREVIOUS PAGES This eighteenth-century blue paste paper has been decorated with implements such as combs, as well as the binder's thumb.

LEFT This paper has been brushed with red paste and then blocked with a simple pattern.

OPPOSITE This pattern
has been made with
woodblock and paste
paint.

ABOVE The wave pattern
here has been made with
a special comb or rake.

OPPOSITE This nineteenth-century woodblock design has been printed on a red paste paper background.

The author would like to thank the following for their help in producing *Treasures in Focus: Decorated Papers*: John Goldfinch and Gillian Ridgley.

All images are taken from the Olga Hirsch collection in the British Library:

p. 1 J3409a; pp.2-3 J153; p. 6 J335; p. 8 *Diario Ecclesiastico par a o Reino de Portugal* (Lisbon, 1818), BJ1a; p. 10 Ernest Fouinet, *L'île des cinq* (Tours, 1885), BJ21; p. 11 J2386; p. 13 J3561; pp. 16-17 J340; p. 19 J334; p. 20 BJ3; p. 22 J337; p. 23 Niccolò Garteromaco, *Il Ricciardetto* (Orleans, 1785), BJ4; p. 24 *Evangelisches Gesang-Buch* (Breslau, 1790), B16; p. 25 J3455a; p.26 J969; p. 27 J876; p. 28 J3409a; p. 29 J3457a; pp. 30-31 J136; p. 33 J7; p. 34 J281; p. 35 J319; pp. 36-37 J44; p. 38 J321; p. 39 J130; p. 40 J247; p. 42 J212; p. 43 J3379; pp. 44-45 J1691; p. 48 Kürfursten Stammbuch, 1604, B2; p. 49 J1492; p. 51 Jacob van der Heyden, *Speculum Cornelianum* (Strasbourg, 1618), B3; p. 52 J1890; p. 53 J1908; p. 54 J1795; p. 55 J1898; pp. 56-57 J2354; p. 59 J2373; p. 60 J339; p. 61 J2356; p. 62 BJ65

First published 2007 by
The British Library
96 Euston Road
London
NW1 2DB

British Library cataloguing in Publication Data
A catalogue record for this book is available from
The British Library

ISBN 978 0 7123 0950 9

Designed and typeset in Berkeley by Bobby & Co, London
Colour reproductions by Dot Gradations Ltd, UK
Printed in Italy by Printer Trento S.r.l.